D1196084

The
Alphabet of Civility

By Virginia Clark Clarkson
Illustrated by Cynthia Vehslage

For_____

From _____

Starrhill Press
Washington & Philadelphia

Published by Starrhill Press, Inc.
P.O. Box 32342, Washington, DC 20007
Telephone (202) 686-6703

Text copyright © 1993, Virginia Clark Clarkson
Illustrations copyright © 1993, Cynthia Vehslage
All rights reserved.

Library of Congress Cataloging-in-Publication Data

Clarkson, Virginia Clark. 1926-
    The alphabet of civility / by Virginia Clark Clarkson :
  illustrated by Cynthia Vehslage.
      p.   cm.
    Summary: An alphabet book emphasizing the value of honesty,
  generosity, humor, promptness, self-respect, and respecting others.
    ISBN 0-913515-86-8
    1. Children--Conduct of life. 2. English language--Alphabet-
  - Juvenile literature. [1. Conduct of life. 2. Alphabet.]
  I. Vehslage, Cynthia, ill. II. Title.
  BJ1631.C53 1993
  170'.83[E]--dc20   93-16586
                                       CIP
                                       AC

Printed in Mexico
1 2 3 4 5 6 7 8 9

For
Laëtia, Matthew, Schuyler,
Emily, Whitney Leigh,
Elena . . .

and YOU

Always keep it
  if you promise.

Always return it
  if you borrow.

BE
ON
TIME

You on time
keeps the other person from
feeling tight and terrible.

Children
who are younger than you
sometimes need kids like you
to help.

Different
    is a nice change
        from Same.
It doesn't mean better or worse
It means Interesting.

Eat a little bit of
everything on your plate.

It doesn't hurt you
and it makes the chef feel good.

Flashlights
are good to have by your bed . . .

If someone needs you in the night,
you can Find them.

Give away
anything you don't use
if you don't love it too much.

Hug BIG.

Hug TIGHT.

Hug OFTEN.

IN doors is shelter.
IN bed is cozy.
IN a bad mood is not fun.
INside-out is confusing.
INvited is a party.

Jokes
        Teasing
                and Giggles
are good for the funny bone.

Which is why it is called the HUMOROUS.

Keep your eyes open.
Keep your ears pricked.
Keep your nose twitching.
Keep your fingers feeling.

The more they tell you, the more you Know.

aLone can be a good thing.

It gives you time for
thinking . . .
wishing . . .
singing . . .
dancing . . .
reading . . .
imagining . . .

MAKE any presents
that you give
to your grown-up
relatives.

It will please them
more than anything.

Never ever
say or do
a mean thing
on purpose.

O

R

Is

havinG

your own Ideas

and tryiNg them out.

A

L

Parents
can be fun.

Enjoy at least one
every day.

Quiet is not a bad thing,
especially
if someone else is
working
or sleeping.

sh . . .   shh . . .   shhh . . .

Running out can be awful.
For instance, running out of
cookies, or tooth paste,
or crayons, or books to read,
or something to do.

But running out in the rain
is wonderful and wet.

Secrets should be Secret,
told only to the Secreter
and
the Secretee.

Try these Top Ten Terrific sayings:
Hello.
Please.
Thank you.
I'm sorry.
Good job!
LeT me help you.
You look nice.
Can you show me how to do ThaT?
Here, have some of mine.
I love you...

You
deserve any praises
and all the compliments
you get.

Enjoy them.

Visit
your relatives
and other great places
whenever you get
the chance.

The World is our living place.
We must take care of it,
the birds and trees
and snakes and bugs
and flowers and fish and people
and water and air.

Have we forgotten anything?

EXplain
when you disagree.

Then
maybe
the other person
will understand.

WhY? WhY? Keep asking WhY?
WhY does your body get limp
    if you don't eat or drink?
WhY does your brain get goofy
    if you don't exercise?
WhY is it that if you're not neat,
    you are a MESS?

Whether you are
a Zinnia
a Zebra, or
a Zorilla . . .
life is a Zillion times
more exciting
if you join in and have fun!

Zap!　　　Zip!

There is much, much more
to think about. Unfortunately,
our ALPHABET
has only 26 letters.

Sorry
that's just
the way
it is.